YOUR KNOWLEDGE HAS VALUE

- We will publish your bachelor's and master's thesis, essays and papers

- Your own eBook and book - sold worldwide in all relevant shops

- Earn money with each sale

Upload your text at www.GRIN.com and publish for free

Bibliographic information published by the German National Library:

The German National Library lists this publication in the National Bibliography; detailed bibliographic data are available on the Internet at http://dnb.dnb.de .

This book is copyright material and must not be copied, reproduced, transferred, distributed, leased, licensed or publicly performed or used in any way except as specifically permitted in writing by the publishers, as allowed under the terms and conditions under which it was purchased or as strictly permitted by applicable copyright law. Any unauthorized distribution or use of this text may be a direct infringement of the author s and publisher s rights and those responsible may be liable in law accordingly.

Imprint:

Copyright © 2015 GRIN Verlag, Open Publishing GmbH
Print and binding: Books on Demand GmbH, Norderstedt Germany
ISBN: 9783668458659

This book at GRIN:

http://www.grin.com/en/e-book/367240/children-s-literature-the-controversy-in-judy-blume-s-are-you-there-god

Phyllis Economy

Children's Literature. The Controversy in Judy Blume's "Are You There God? It's Me Margaret"

GRIN Publishing

GRIN - Your knowledge has value

Since its foundation in 1998, GRIN has specialized in publishing academic texts by students, college teachers and other academics as e-book and printed book. The website www.grin.com is an ideal platform for presenting term papers, final papers, scientific essays, dissertations and specialist books.

Visit us on the internet:

http://www.grin.com/

http://www.facebook.com/grincom

http://www.twitter.com/grin_com

Controversy in *Are you there God? It's me Margaret*

Phyllis Economy

Winthrop University

Content

Introduction 2
Evaluation 2
Controversial Issues 5
    Issue one 6
    Issue two 7
Final Decision 8
Conclusion 9
References 10

Introduction

The book *Are You there God? It's me Margaret,* by Judy Blume (1970), takes on a humorous and insightful journey through the pubescent stage of twelve year old Margaret Simon's life. We hear all her private thoughts about what goes on in her life and what she would rather happen in her life. While Blume's book, *Are You there God? It's me Margaret,* is an profound and comical read for pre-teen girls, I believe that students in fifth grade and higher should be able to read the book. While the language of the book is simple for the reading level of a third grader (Titlewave), the content is too mature for them and should be selected for older, preteen students who understand and are in the midst of going through those stages in life.

Margaret's issues are presented in a straightforward and blunt manner. She is conflicted between choosing her own religion, but just ends up talking to God. She talks and prays to Him daily about whatever is on her mind. The issues of boys, kissing, and sexuality are present throughout the book (Blume 1970). Margaret is infatuated with her body and is constantly thinking about when her body is going to develop like her other friends. She prays to God for her menstrual cycle to start and for her chest to grow, all typical pre-teen girl thoughts (Blume, 1970). However, these controversial life experience's that Margaret goes through and documents (Blume, 1970), are seen as inappropriate for some readers, but as reassurances to older readers.

Evaluation

According to Kiefer and Tyson (2014), a contemporary realistic fiction book should allow the reader to relate to the characters and the situations that are presented in the book. In Blume's (1970) book, *Are You There God? It's Me Margaret*, the readers go on a personal journey with Margaret and experience all the trials and tribulations of being a sixth grade girl in a new school. Margaret is honestly portrayed as a happy-go-lucky pre-teen who has to move to New Jersey with her mom and dad. We hear her quirky thoughts about how unfortunate it is to have to be uprooted from the place that you know and to start fresh in a school with new people and have to deal with growing up all in the same year. Throughout the book the controversial themes of believing in God and having a defined religion, as well as going through puberty, beginner bras and getting your first menstrual cycle, are clearly discussed in detail. Blume writes straightforwardly about what is going on through a middle school girls' life and how exciting, but nerve-racking it can be.

In the book (Blume, 1970), Margaret constantly talks to God in times of need, questioning His powers and praying for her body to start developing naturally like all of her new friends. After meeting up with her friends and reciting their group chant-exercise of "We must-we must-we must increase our bust!" (p. 72), Margaret comes home and convinces her mother to go to the store to buy her a bra. She then prays, "Are you there God? It's me, Margaret. I just told my mother I want a bra. Please help me grow God. You know where" (p. 37). Margaret finds a certain solace in talking to God, and I think many middle school girls can relate to that feeling when they talk to someone older who they know will not judge them. Margaret is also focused on getting her period. Margaret makes friends with a few girls in her new class and, in typical middle school fashion, they develop a girl group with secret names, books, and a period pact. These girls are all very credible middle school girl characters. In her girl group, there is the 'leader' Nancy, who does not have a problem bragging about her development and knowledge about periods.

Margaret also is faced with the choice of believing in God from a Jewish or a Christian standpoint. Margaret blatantly tells her new friends about her parents' scandalous elopement and how they decided to not raise her a certain faith over the other, they would let her decide what she believes when she is old enough. She tells God her deepest thoughts, but feels comfortable when talking to him, begging Him to make her be "normal" (p. 100). She even prays to have Him help her find her religion, "I'm more confused than ever…Which religion should I be? Sometimes I wish I'd been born one way or the other" (p. 94). Throughout the book, Margaret tries out different churches in her journey of trying to find God. After each service, Margaret prays to God and tells him what she liked, but always that she did not fully feel His presence. It is not until she gets her period when she realizes that, "I know you're there God. I know you wouldn't have missed this for anything!" (p. 149). I believe this is an honest portrayal of how a middle school girl would feel if she was going through the process of believing in God, or anything.

    I feel as if Blume does an excellent job in representing the true experience of a curious middle school girl going through puberty and trying to find her true beliefs. While this book does present controversial issues that maybe some middle-school girls would be uncomfortable reading about, it shows young girls that they are not the only ones out there that are experiencing these thoughts (Syzmanski, 2007). Through Margaret's experiences and prayers, middle school girls can read this and make their own connections with some of the issues they are faced with and see how Margaret handles them. This book fulfills Kiefer and Tyson's (2014) description on a contemporary realistic fiction book because it shows the reader another perspective that might seem comforting for the age group.

Controversial Issues

There are themes throughout the book that are controversial for some readers. Any children's book that deals with religious beliefs always attracts both positive and negative attention (Brewbaker, 1983). She prays to God daily because she finds comfort in telling him all her secret thoughts and asks Him for guidance as she struggles with choosing her exact religious beliefs. After attempting a Catholic church ritual of confession, that did not live up to her standards, Margaret prays, "I looked for you when I wanted to confess. But you weren't there. I didn't feel you at all. Not the way I do when I talk to you at night. Why God? Why do I only feel you when I'm alone?" (Blume, p.120). Margaret's parents, being raised in two very different religious households, chose not to raise her a certain way. Instead, they decided to let her choose her religion when she is old enough. However, contradictory to her parents' decisions, Margaret is faced with two sets of grandparents who believe it is important she choose a religion and sometimes take matters into their own hands (Blume 1970). The book highlights the fact that "Margaret finds that pressures from loving grandparents, Jewish on one side and Christian on the other, can make the business of choosing a religion pretty distasteful" (Brewbaker, 1983). Other controversial issues that are presented in the book (Blume 1970) are boys, first kisses, and expressions of sexuality. Margaret's new friend Nancy brings up the fact numerous times that boys are only interested in "pictures of naked girls and dirty books" (p.11). Margaret even brings her dad's copy of Playboy to one of her girl group meetings to look at the centerfold's chest (Blume, 1970). Another controversial issue that is prominent in the entire book is female body development: "Menstruation lies at the center of Margaret's world and her thoughts are monopolized by anxiety about when her period will come, how it will happen, and what it will feel like" (Szymanski, p.3). All the issues can be seen as controversial in the classroom, but are not harmful for student's to read about and understand. In the following sections, the issues of religion and female body development will be analyzed deeper.

Issue one In the book (Blume, 1970), even stemming from the title, God's existence plays a major role. Margaret explains to the reader that, "[She doesn't] think a person can decide to be a certain religion like that. It's like having to choose your own name" (Blume, p. 143). She battles choosing her religion, Christian or Jewish, and even her belief that there is a God; she even fluctuates towards the end of the book questioning God's existence, before having an epiphany that resolves her question (Blume, 1970). She has to deal with her Jewish grandmother, whom she is very close with, always questioning if she has made up her mind. Margaret asks herself, "As long as she loves me and I love her, what difference does religion make?" (Blume, p. 141). While this issue may seem uneasy for some to have their children read, the fact of the matter is, that children have these questions and it is important that they know they are not alone and that it is okay to feel the need to talk about it and even question it (Brewbaker, 1983). Margaret constantly prays for God to give her some kind of guidance about what religious path she should take, as well as for her body to grow and boys to like her; she finds comfort knowing God is there to talk to (Blume, 1970). According to Brewbaker (1983), "In these novels, experience is the predominant teacher as young characters gain insight into their problems through living through them and, more often than not, facing their consequences" (p. 84). Documented by Banned Book Awareness (2003), it was challenged in Ohio at school libraries because of the "anti-Christian behavior" and thoughts (2003). The book (1970), was also challenged at one point in both Alabama and Wisconsin (Banned Book Awareness, 2003). It is important for children to discover and ask questions, regardless of what the issue is. If they have a certain level of maturity and are in a time of their life where they are starting to wonder about these issues, books like this are imperative for them to read and take comfort in (Brewbaker, 1983, p. 86).

Issue two While Margaret's belief in God is a major part of the book, female body development is another one of her great conflicting issues. Blume (1970) shows the most vulnerable thoughts of a preteen girl who spends her days questioning when her body is going to be normal and develop like all of her friends. From the beginning, Margaret is faced with her future friend Nancy exclaiming, "Oh, you're still flat" (Blume, p.7). The girls make a pact that they must all wear bras, even if they have not developed at all. Margaret's embarrassed feelings are laid out in the book and she even stuffs her bra for a party in hopes of getting more attention from her friends and from boys (Blume, 1970). The girls are also concerned with when their period will start and why it has not already. The girls practice using feminine napkins and wear them to try and get comfortable (Blume, 1970). The story explores the emotions of young girls going through puberty and sheds light on the various questions young girls may have (Szymanski, 2007). Even though this may be uncomfortable for parents to allow their children to read or for teachers to keep in their classroom, the fact is that "Puberty is a common human experience, one that is not often publicly addressed but that happens to everyone" (Szymanski, 2007) and young girls will have questions about it. Many pre-teen girls go through the feeling of embarrassment if they are not as well-endowed or have not had their period like their friends have. This book (Blume, 1970) serves "as a safe, honest form of communication to adolescents, letting them them know that puberty *is* confusing and it *is* different for everyone, but that they are not alone" (Szymanski, 2007). According to Banned Books Awareness (2003), a few Montana school libraries challenged the book due to the sexual content, but the challenge was dropped and it stayed in the libraries. The explicit talk about the female body development and menstrual cycle is the main subject matter of the book that has caused it to be challenged and banned in certain areas because of "Blume's frank discussion of these issues (Syzamanski, p. 3)."

Final Decision

Are You there God? It's me Margaret (1970), should definitely not be banned. The book provides a relief for young girls who are going through puberty (Syzamanski, 2007), (Banned Books Awareness, 2003). As Blume herself stated in an interview, "We don't want to acknowledge them for very one very selfish reason: they make us uncomfortable" (as cited in Banned Books Awareness, 2003). If parents or teachers continue to hoard these books away from their children thinking they are doing them a favor so they will not be exposed to the explicit content, they are instead doing them harm. Children learn from reading or hearing about other perspectives, and they need to be able to ask questions just like Margaret does in the book (Blume, 1970). In an experimental interview with students conducted by Isajlovic-Terry and McKechnie (2012) regarding the students' views on censorship, one student proclaimed she believed that children should be able to "to read whatever they want and believe in whatever they feel like believing in" (p. 40). Many other students in the interview (Isajlovic-Terry and McKechnie, 2012) believed that books should rather be "limit[ed]" (p.40) to older students, but not completely wiped out of the library. A great use for this book, with both male and female students would be to focus on the religion segments and use them as a discussion. This will show diversity in the classroom that some students may not be aware of. Reading is how students understand and widen their horizons. This book would be a great choice to use for a small group of all girls. They would really be able to relate and discuss these topics from their own points of view. This in turn, would show the group similarities and differences on what girls go through during puberty. Young girls need to have that snapshot into Margaret's mind to see that they are not alone in the questions they have about what their body is going through. As Szymanski (2007) writes, "Few other stages in life are as universal as puberty" (p. 3) and that is why it a necessity to not keep it covered, but to talk about it and get young girls more knowledgeable and less timid about it.

Conclusion

While this book contains many controversial issues that may seem uncomfortable for teachers and parents to allow children to read, it is a well written book that middle school students could gain a lot from reading (Brewbaker, 1983), (Kiefer and Tyson, 2014), (Szymanski, 2007). I believe this book is an informative and important read for preteen girls. This book gives them the comfort that every girl goes through the same thing they are and it is okay to be nervous about it. However, while the third grade reading level is too low (Titlewave), *Are You there God? It's me Margaret* (1970) should not be banned from older students who are more likely to gain insight and relief from reading the book.

References

Banned Books Awareness. (2003, November). *Are you there God? It's me, Margaret*. Retrieved from http://bannedbooks.world.edu/2013/11/03/banned-books-awareness-are-you-there-god-its-me-margaret/.

Brewbaker, J. (1983). Young Adult Literature: Are you there, Margaret? It's me, God—religious contexts in recent adolescent fiction. *The English Journal 72*(5), 82-86.

Blume J. (1970). *Are you there God? It's me Margaret.* New York City: Atheneum Books for Young Readers.

Isajlovic-Terry, N. & McKechnie, L. (2012). An Exploratory Study of Children's Views of Censorship. *Children and Libraries.* 38-43.

Kiefer, B., & Tyson, C. (2014). *Charlotte Huck's children's literature: A brief guide* (2nd Ed.). New York: McGraw-Hill.

Szymanski, M. (2007, Spring/Summer). Adolescence, literature and censorship: Unpacking the controversy surrounding Judy Blume. *NeoAmericanist 3*(1), 1-10.

Titlwave. (n.d.). *Are you there God? It's me Margaret*. Retrieved from http://www.titlewave.com/search?SID=fd8d050bfdfd94f78d1ec20c3db42acb#I2.

YOUR KNOWLEDGE HAS VALUE

- We will publish your bachelor's and master's thesis, essays and papers

- Your own eBook and book - sold worldwide in all relevant shops

- Earn money with each sale

Upload your text at www.GRIN.com and publish for free